The Caged Bird With 'Clipped' Wings

Daniel Garza

BookLeaf Publishing

India | USA | UK

Presentation by *BookLeaf Publishing*

Web: www.bookleafpub.com

E-mail: info@bookleafpub.com

ISBN: 9789358318982

First edition 2024

ACKNOWLEDGEMENT

Thank you to those bold enough to join me on this part of the journey by reading on. Also, I would like to thank the man in the mirror for eliminating all self-hate by daily reminding me to *be no less than great.* On purpose, with purpose. One love.

PREFACE

The job of a healer is to help you find your own power, not to make you dependent on theirs.

The Caged Bird With 'Clipped' Wings

Even **with 'clipped' WINGS**,
With all its heart, a **caged bird** SINGS,
Because it loves the joy that to himself, it
BRINGS.

He peeps, chirps, and TWEETS,
About how his own worst enemy he daily
BEATS,
To the demons he DEFEATS,
And to death, since 'it', he repeatedly CHEATS.

Despite his voice sometimes being a bit off or
BROKEN,
His tune is still sung or SPOKEN.
He is not after the TOKEN!

This caged bird just flies freely when his song,
he SINGS.
It does not matter that he is 'missing' parts of his
WINGS.
Because the beat[s] in his heart is where
happiness BEGINS,
And he can't help but feel joy from the freedom
it BRINGS!

A Healing Mans Heart

A healing mans heart has volumes to SPEAK,
About the many many moments he felt WEAK.
And how eternal peace is all it is out to SEEK.

Pages and pages can be fully WRITTEN,
Of the pain inflicted from being repeatedly
BITTEN,

By the serpent's life cycle's deadly DECISION,
To let him inject himself with venomous poison
to cloud his VISION,

Of the all-seeing eye found in his MIND,
That is always connected to Source and helps
him FIND,
A way out of being CONFINED,

To what can be reduced to a mere THOUGHT.
That he has the power to control because he is
NOT,
A ROBOT.

No; Just a simple man with a beautiful soul
because my heart, I *am* HEALING!
That for the first time, I am knowing what I
'thought' I would *never* be FEELING!

The Storm

On the outside, I may look as calm as day but
inside rages on a brutal **STORM.**
One that, at any moment, can take on a different
FORM.

Turbulent thoughts cause for brute force
WINDS.
Images going round and round like a tornado
until my head SPINS.

Thunderous demonic voices thunderously
ROAR.
Echoing inside me, reaching the depths of the
universe's very CORE!

Black clouds full of bad memories threaten to
keep unclear my mind's VISION,

Of my future by wanting to askew my next
DECISION.

Remaining as still as possible, this storm I know
I can also WEATHER,
Just *be* light, *be* like a bird, like a FEATHER.

Tossing And Turning

For many nights I have been **tossing and
TURNING.**
From the hurtful memories inside me
BURNING!
From their pain growing and LEARNING.
For infinite peace, severely YEARNING.

Every night has felt like weeks on END.
That I am okay, I do my best to *not* PRETEND.
Because why lie knowing none of us would
mind having at least one good FRIEND.

This **tossing and turning** has given me little to
no SLEEP.
Or perhaps it's been the huge urge to WEEP.

That, every night, every part of me has had to
OVERCOME.
Because from the depths of my heart is where
the tears are FROM.

The Righteous Path

How do I know that the path I'm on is RIGHT?
Is it with what I do during the day or the last
thought I have before I go to sleep at NIGHT?

I watch out for the SIGNS.
I don't want to step on any past landMINES!

I could blow up or off my LEGS.
Sometimes it feels like I'm walking on the shells
of EGGS!

How do I confirm I am fulfilling my soul's
PURPOSE?
Am I showing my deepest self or just what's on
the SURFACE?

How often and by whom is judged the purity of
my HEART?
When and who gets to decide when my
righteous path is to officially START?

Tainted Memories

An image of the wars with the darkness inside
me, let me PAINT.
It's a bit graphic, so it's *NOT* for those with a
heart that's FAINT.
Demons daily do their best to my heart and its
good intentions **TAINT**,
With **memories** of myself when I wasn't such a
SAINT.

It's like witnessing a constant hemorrhage of my
own brain by always seeing so much BLOOD.
To drown me in sorrow, with pictures of our
crying mothers, my mind they continuously
FLOOD.

The sounds of gunshots ringing in my EARS.
The empty expression on the faces of my several
passed PEERS.
This has happened over and over for many,
many YEARS.

Repeatedly, there is a brutal FIGHT,
As they desperately want to extinguish my
LIGHT,
By intending to drag me back into my darkest
NIGHT.
But I hold onto my heart really really TIGHT!

And stay true to the power within us all that is
good, to then *be* GREATER.
Because we are ***ALL*** just an extension of our
divine CREATOR.

Silent Suffering

When in **silence** you **SUFFER,**
Your heart may get a little TOUGHER,
But makes for a life a whole lot ROUGHER.

You walk amongst the 'living' with a dead
SPIRIT.
And you know this because your eyes scream in
pain but no one seems to hear IT!

Everyday you are the pallbearer and witness of a
funeral that is your OWN.
You see your body withering down to the
BONE.

Soon after you lower the 'dead' parts of yourself
into the imaginary GRAVE,

You pray for your peace and for the strength so that what's left of you, you continue doing *your* best to SAVE.

Stolen Joy

I do my best to feel even a little **JOY.**
But there is the image of that grown BOY,

That carries something heavy on each
SHOULDER.
That is slowly sinking him to the bottom as he
grows OLDER.

I do my best to swim back up to take another
BREATH.
Because drowning alive can't be his physical
DEATH.

I do my best to a little joy FEEL!
Before 'the reaper' comes again, to it **STEAL**.

Fade Away

Sometimes, these beautiful images full of colors
bouncing around in my mind, begin to slowly
FADE.
Then there are moments when everything has
become instantly GRAYED.

Nothing to the left. Nothing to the right. All is
DULL.
Just the inside walls of a plain old SKULL.

All of a sudden, I find myself in the midst of
nothing to ENJOY.
Somehow only seeing flashes of that tormented
hurt little BOY.

Then quick projections of the many expressions
of me suffering up until NOW.
To still have Life after going through so much
anguish even has the darkest of demons asking,
"HOW?"
But also Angels of light applauding and yelling,
"WOW!"

So to them I silently and continuously PRAY,
Every single DAY,

Until the colours and my smile return as the darkness begins to **fade AWAY.**

Burning At The Stake

In a nightmare I had, a dark part of my mind had
my heart tightly tied to a **STAKE.**
My spirit, it desperately wants to BREAK.

I see my heart looking down bravely at the
FLAMES.
Demonic silhouettes behind them calling it
shameful NAMES.

Their hateful words **burning** worse than the
FIRE.
Intending to reach deep into my most desirable
DESIRE.

To the integrity of its good intentions, my heart
holds STEADY.
To die honorably defending it, I am always
READY.

As their curses grew louder, with more intensity
the fire began to BURN.
Every thought became more and more malicious
as each one took their TURN.

Pushing out from the depths of my core, I felt
the painful SCREAM.

Thankfully, before it came out, I awoke from
that dreadful DREAM.

My Behavior

Of emotions, I get hit with a big WAVE.
Parts of me don't know how to BEHAVE.
My thoughts threaten to turn me into their
SLAVE.

I feel myself taking a deep breath to keep
oxygen in my LUNGS.
The voice[s] in my head are now speaking in
TONGUES.

My balance, I feel I'm beginning to LOSE.
And a bit of my faith as well, so what to do next
I must carefully CHOOSE.

How to act in such dire CIRCUMSTANCES?
That it be irrational, high are the CHANCES!

To BE present with all that I am feeling, I
continue doing my BEST.
So I steady the rise, fall and beats of my CHEST.

I am the only one responsible for **my
BEHAVIOR.**
As I *am* my one and only SAVIOR.

Difficult

It's been a bit **difficult** to keep myself AFLOAT.
With heavy stones from the past, these demons
have been rocking my present BOAT.

They've been threatening to tip me
OVERBOARD.
This has happened daily as higher and higher
I've SOARED.

It's been a bit **difficult** to breathe STEADILY.
To tune into the birds chirping their beautiful
MELODY.

It's even been a bit **difficult** to PRAY.
To feel Faith that the Sun is *still* shining when
the clouds make the sky GRAY.

Lately, it's been **difficult** to laugh and also CRY.
Either we do or don't, there is no TRY.

This poem, **difficult** to write, it was quite a BIT.
But I will have, once again, emerged stronger
from the bottom of the PIT.

No Denial Of Love And A Smile

When I see the bright smile I still get to create
on my wonderful FACE,
I can't help but be inspired to open my heart to
free up more SPACE,

So I can make room for more joy even through
all the pain I've caused it by giving away, my
trust, so MUCH.
Becoming so sensitive, even to the slightest of
TOUCH.

But because the happiness I feel, only *IT* gets to
DICTATE,
It repeatedly reminds me that, about me and Life
there is *nothing* to HATE.

And that in fact, to *being* Love, an unlimited
amount I *can* WILL.
Which is with what, all of me I daily RE-FILL.

So as much as possible, I let myself honorably
wear that beautiful luminous **SMILE**,
Because that I *am* worthy of giving myself pure
unconditional **love**, there IS **no DENIAL**.

At The Mercy Of

Sometimes I find myself **at the mercy of** some
demonic VOICES.
'They' haggle me about my past CHOICES.

In my head, very CLEAR,
'them' I can HEAR.
And find myself **at the mercy of** shedding many
a TEAR.

For what 'they' say has quite the STING.
And a throbbing pain to my heart 'they' BRING.

I do my best to innerstand 'their' INTENTION.
I look deep deep into my own REFLECTION.

I then ask myself, "What am I **at the mercy
OF??"**
"Not showing yourself, unconditional LOVE!"

Magical Dust

Each individual star has its own luminescent
POWER.
Sometimes a cluster of them fall and our space
they SHOWER.

Some break through the atmosphere and reach
the EARTH.
With each one's demise comes another's BIRTH.

They illuminate the eyes and a path for those of
us who shoot to be one of THEM.
But instead, end up in the dark, time and time
AGAIN.

But our aim we simply RE-ADJUST.
In our faith, put all of our TRUST.
Because we are eternal and made up of the same
magical DUST.

Heard

For those of you who feel you aren't being
HEARD,
Please remember that there is not only one, but
many a BIRD.

Each one happily chirping its little lungs and
heart AWAY,
at the crack of dawn, during and the descending
of each DAY.

Never caring, never knowing that while It
gleefully delivers its TUNE,
you can find the Sun, the Stars and the MOON,

enjoying and appreciating that they've gotten to
hear such a delightful SONG.
The winds joyfully spreading each one across
world[s] all day LONG.

So let your voice also be one of those being
HEARD.
And remember someone IS always listening, so
like the birds, let out a many good WORD.

Smile For Life

A **smile** brings much JOY.
Whether it's from a girl or a BOY.
Its joyfulness is meant for everyone to ENJOY.

To bring one out from everyone doesn't take
MUCH.
The right part of the heart just needs the slightest
TOUCH.

And that can come from a single, simple
THOUGHT.
That we have the choice to have because we
aren't anyone's ROBOT.
So go ahead, why NOT??

Right NOW think of what will make you and
others **SMILE**.
And hold it for a Loooong WHILE,
Until it becomes a **LIFESTYLE**.

Shaken

Sometimes I find my faith being **SHAKEN**
As soon as I AWAKEN.

When, to the light within me, I begin to
ADJUST,
Doubt quickly grows where there is supposed to
be unmovable TRUST.

Sometimes my faith is being **SHAKEN**
By malicious voices loudly repeating that I have
been MISTAKEN,

In thinking I am *incapable* of BREAKING.
Along with my faith, I feel the rest of myself
uncontrollably SHAKING.

But I guess I haven't completely broken apart
YET,

Because an opportunity to me wholeheartedly
write these words and *you* read them, we are
again blessed to GET.

Taking The Place Of The Sun

I had to **take the place of the Sun** TODAY,
As the clouds were nastily thick and GRAY,
Relentlessly blocking its WAY.

Although it seemed it was to be a day of
GLOOM,
That for happiness, there would be no ROOM,
Here I come like a lotus flower in full BLOOM.

To the mood of many, those dark clouds posed a
THREAT.
Make some feel UPSET,
While others FRET.
But with me, their match, they MET.

Because their darkness is not MINE.
Therefore, my way of being, they cannot
DEFINE.
And as we are all part of the same DIVINE,

I still possess the power to SHINE.

And so today I **took the place of the SUN.**
From such an honor, no way I would RUN.
Because putting smiles on peoples faces is so
much FUN.
And hey, to do the same, *you* too can be the
ONE.

Set Free

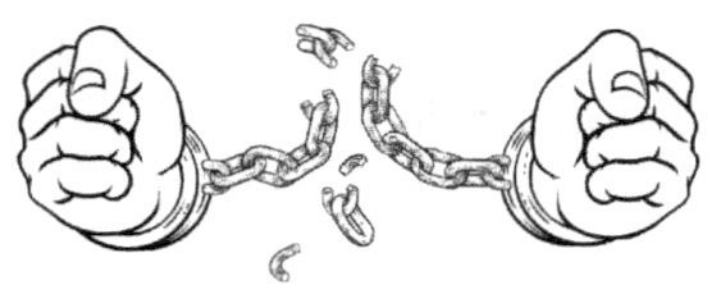

Why do we talk about what COULD,
WOULD,
And SHOULD,

Have happened, as if it CAN,
Actually change the original PLAN,
More THAN,

How it, *already* WENT?
How the 'time' was already SPENT?
Not accepting that it was MEANT,

To be that WAY.
That whole DAY.
No matter what we do nor SAY,
It will still STAY,

In the PAST.
In your memory LAST,
infinitely or dissipate just as FAST.

It's all in your HANDS,

And head for who UNDERSTANDS,
That we have pineal GLANDS,

That help you SEE,
What was, *IS* and will BE.
And that will **set** you **FREE.**

Different

As I look at the world around me, Eye see that **different** is MY point of VIEW.
I see the difference between me and YOU.

But then I don't because we are one and the
SAME,
Even if **different** is our NAME.

Even if you were birthed in a **different** PLACE,
Or what has been deemed a **different** RACE.
Because the smile on your FACE,

Isn't **different** from the one on MINE.
Yes; We are all just as DIVINE.

So as Eye view the world around me, I notice
that what is **different** is just my
PERSPECTIVE.
I then ask myself if the best version of me, to
you, am I being REFLECTIVE?

Why

Why does my heart still BEAT,
If I can barely stand on my FEET?

Why does my mind still want to have happy
THOUGHTS,
If I can see dead SPOTS?

Why do I still feel like pushing ON,
When I feel most of my soul's GONE?

Why do I still FIGHT,
If I can barely see the LIGHT?

Why do my lungs still take another BREATHE,
If there is so much *peace* during DEATH!

Making My Way

For me, there was no laid out path with set
TRACKS.
So my entire state of being is tired from
swinging the pick, the machete, the shovel and
the AX.
I've steadily been making my way through this
jungle of life without a moment to RELAX.

There have been many days of endless RAIN.
From the snake bites, falls, thorns, and lost ways
there has been tremendous PAIN.

There have been many nights without SLEEP.
Into the collective consciousness, my blood and
tears infinitely SEEP.
But I get to decide which version[s] of me to
KEEP.

So I will continue **making my way** doing
exactly as I MUST.
In the power of my own faith in divine timing,
I put all my TRUST,
Because life is JUST.

Delusional

Am I **delusional** for 'thinking' we can ALL
actually get ALONG?
I feel we may have been looking at Life all
WRONG.

Am I **delusional** for wanting everyone to, at
peace, always BE?
I know it's not only ME,

Filled with these beautiful 'thoughts' about life
that make up this clear VISION.
That to see, all it takes is to make a different
DECISION,

From the infinite ones that our Creator to us,
moment by passing moment, it PRESENTS.
I know I am not **delusional** as I ALWAYS feel
its power within my PRESENCE.

Thriver Vs Survivor

I am NOW identifying myself as a **THRIVER**,
Not just another **SURVIVOR**.

Tremendous have been the GAINS.
"You had to go through the growing PAINS!",
My Spirit EXPLAINS...

I am NOW going to take all the HURT,
Transmute it and with love, my emotions
BLURT,
Because at speaking from the heart, I am an
EXPERT.

About healing, is all I will allow my mouth to
TALK.
Down the beaten path, I will not allow my feet
to WALK.
I will do my best to stay grounded like a ROCK.

Solid and adaptable to its SURROUNDINGS.
I will continuously broadcast my FINDINGS,

Of where to go to unEarth daily PEACE.
So from your heart, all suffering, you too, will
RELEASE.